TRACK AND FIELD

TRACK AND FIELD

BY JOHN AND FRANCES CRAIG

FRANKLIN WATTS
NEW YORK / LONDON / 1979
A FIRST BOOK

Cover photograph courtesy of: Leo deWys, Inc.

Photographs courtesy of: Lorraine Rorke:
pp. 6 (left), 22 (bottom), 25, 26, 37, 57;
Sygma (Jean-Pierre Laffont): pp. 6 (right),
48 (left); Sygma (Alain DeJean): pp. 17,
22 (top); United Press International: pp.
11, 48 (right); Wide World Photos: p. 54.

Library of Congress Cataloging
in Publication Data

Craig, John, 1921–
Track and field.

(A First book)
Bibliography: p.
Includes index.
SUMMARY: Introduces the basic track and field
events and advises would-be athletes on prepar-
ing for these sports.

1. Track-athletics—Juvenile literature. [1. Track
and field] I. Craig, Frances, joint author. II. Title.
GV1060.5.C67   796.4'2   78–23180
ISBN 0–531–02264–1

CONTENTS

TRACK AND FIELD

TRACK AND FIELD

Track and field (or athletics) is probably the oldest "sport" in the world. Long before the beginning of recorded history, young men and women had to run fast, jump high and far, and throw hard—if only to obtain the food that their people required and to protect themselves from their enemies.

It is also as "new" as the latest world record.

And as modern as the next Olympic Games, scheduled for Moscow in the summer of 1980.

It involves millions of athletes of all races, nationalities, ages, and personalities—men and women, boys and girls, "masters" in their sixties and seventies, toddlers of five and six . . . who only "yesterday" first learned to walk.

There is a place for everyone who wants to be healthy and keep their bodies in good condition.

But track and field means more than trying to outrun, outjump, and outthrow other competitors. It means struggling with fatigued limbs and a heaving chest to go one step further than you thought you could go. It means coaxing one more throw out of an exhausted arm or digging into a weary soul for the strength to make one more jump.

Because most of all, track and field is a venture that goes beyond one's normal limits, into a land of excellence and idealism. For any victory is hollow if it is easily won, and winning lies in the struggle, not in the achievement.

Then comes the thrill of competition, the crowds, noise, excitement. The joy of victory, the agony of defeat.

But the agony is only temporary. You know you did your best—and you know you'll do better another day.

That's track and field.

INTRODUCING THE SPORT

In the open air in the afternoon sun or under the bright lights of evening, a track and field stadium is an exciting place to be. A constantly moving panorama spreads out from mid-field to the peripheral track and up into the seats; it is almost like being at a circus—there are so many things to watch at the same time.

National flags are flying at one end of the stadium, and school and college banners are blowing overhead in the wind. Some ardent fans have brought buntings and streamers and have spread them out over the front railings. The uniforms, and even the shoes of the athletes, are bright and gay, the reds, greens, and yellows contrasting with the bold blacks and whites. And, viewed from one side of the arena to the other, the spectators appear to be thousands of many-hued balloons.

All of the running events at a track and field event take

place on an oval-shaped track, the stadium being wrapped around its outer edge. Here the sprinters crowd several years of training into a few brief moments of competition, while the distance runners maintain the audience's attention for a much longer time, bringing the crowd to its feet with swift bursts and constantly changing positions.

There is much going on in the area inside the track. The announcer, sitting at a table draped with banners, tells the audience something about each of the men and women participating, announces the events, calls the competitors to the marshaling area prior to starting time, and broadcasts the results as they arrive at his desk.

The officials responsible for looking after entries and results are situated in a tent, which protects their papers from the breezes that might send them skyward, or, at least, out of arm's reach. Scattered around the field are clerks, judges, starters, marshals, and timers, working alone or in small groups, performing various duties that keep the events on schedule and the results coming in. These officials are the backbone of any track and field day, giving their interest and time freely and voluntarily, asking for no monetary reward. Sometimes they wear uniforms and walk out together to their positions, adding a bit of drama to the show. They are all part of an organization that can put a thousand bodies, competing in over twenty-five events, in the right places at the right times, with efficiency and consideration.

In the infield there is also a tent for the trainers and doctors. It is there that the athletes' injuries are tended to or, just as important, prevented by the trainers who are specialists in this type of medicine.

There are many contests of physical strength, speed, and endurance occupying this central arena, too. These, of course, are the field events and are usually quite time consuming. The contestants must carefully consider each step to the takeoff board in the jumping events and establish the correct position in the throwing events, keeping warm and relaxed in between turns.

At any one moment at a track and field event there are usually three events being contested. The women's high jump, under way since the start of the day, has been reduced to a few competitors. The men's shot put is just about over, and the athletes in this event—enormous, powerful men—are pacing anxiously in front of the stands. Now, the announcer's voice fills the arena and draws everyone's attention to a spot on the track where the competitors for the one-mile run are being introduced.

As each name is called, a slim athlete jogs forward, stops, and returns to the starting line. Sweat suits are doffed and taken away as the runners concentrate on the task ahead. And, as thousands of spectators, breathless and silent, peer toward the curved white line on the track, a crack from the starter's pistol sends the runners sprinting for the first turn.

Strategy and tactics play major roles in this race, and the winner is not always the fastest runner. Each athlete has studied the competition and has planned a race that will destroy an opponent's strong points. An athlete must be prepared to alter his or her plans as the race unfolds, continually reevaluating the situation at hand.

Meanwhile, the crowd is quiet and filled with tension as it watches a young woman at the high jump. She stands, flexing her leg muscles, clenching and unclenching her hands, then closes her eyes for a moment before she begins her semicircular approach to the bar. Arriving there, she leaps and arches backward, slips over the bar, and lands in t1e

foam-filled pit beyond as an official signals that it is a "good" jump.

And close by, the shot-putters are gearing up for their final throws. As each athlete in this competition jogs restlessly back and forth, he shakes his limbs, trying to stay "loose." Then, stepping into the throwing area with the iron ball, he glides across the circle and heaves the shot with a grunt.

This is a track and field event, where athletes big and small, black and white, male and female, can compete in the same arena; a place where several events, each as dramatic as the next, can be contested at the same time; a sport that combines over forty separate disciplines into one of the greatest challenges and spectacles of the athletic world.

Left: as the field sets up for an event, the timekeeper is ready. Right: the crowd hushes as an Olympic pole-vaulter clears the bar.

BEAUTY AND STRENGTH

". . . what a disgrace it is for a man to grow old without ever seeing the beauty and strength of which his body is capable." When Socrates spoke these words, he was reflecting a sentiment that was common during his time, a sentiment that surrounded the ancient Olympic Games. And although Socrates lived twenty-four hundred years ago, he felt the same admiration for excellence that people all over the world feel today, when the Olympic Games convene every fourth year.

Although archaeologists inform us that ancient Olympics undoubtedly started many centuries before, the first year that the names of the winners were recorded was 776 B.C. Ancient Greece, at the time, was an area of mighty states, and the city of Olympia was beautiful and important. The Olympic festival was something like a fair, with vendors' booths offering art, food, and wine, and poets and artists providing an intellectual balance to the athletics.

The Greeks of those days believed in cultivating the whole man, and young people were educated in athletics as well as in painting, dancing, singing, and the playing of musical instruments. In fact, at a time when athletes were admired for their physical prowess and the beauty of their movements, wars were halted for the Games, and competitors passed, unimpeded, through enemy lines. The first Games were, indeed, a showcase for those with fine moral, intellectual, and physical attributes.

The Greeks admired physical competence for practical reasons. Physical fitness was a requirement for survival in an era when wars were frequent, and a strong, skillful soldier was a successful one. But the Greeks admired fitness for aesthetic reasons also; to them fitness was synonymous with goodness and virility. These early athletic contests were simply a continuation of a part of their way of life.

Competitors in the ancient Games were strict amateurs and were required to answer questions as to their parentage, religion, and character. They also had to provide proof that they had trained for at least ten months prior to the commencement of the contests. And they had to take an oath that they would use no unfair means to win, while officials were sworn to impartiality. Any athlete caught cheating was fined, and a statue was erected as a warning to other athletes that a violation of the amateur code was a personal disgrace.

Running is as old as man, and competitive running is probably as old as civilization itself. A foot race, then, was a natural as the event that began these ancient Games. Originally one length of the stadium, the race was later expanded to two lengths, and then to twelve. The pentathlon had its roots here, too, as running, discus throwing, the javelin, jumping, and wrestling were combined into one competition in an effort to find the best all-round athlete.

The ancient Olympics ended amid corruption and deteriorating standards in 394 A.D., but the Olympic ideals lived on. In 1896, after a break of 1,503 years, a Frenchman named Baron Pierre de Coubertin founded a new Olympic movement. Deeming it proper that the new Games begin in Greece where they originated, de Coubertin initiated the revival of the greatest sporting showcase in the world, and the Olympics have been contested every four years since that inaugural event, with the exception of the years that were torn by the two world wars.

Track and field is still the heart of the Olympic Games, with more athletes taking part in these events than in any other Olympic contest. The arena has changed from a hot and dusty field in Greece to a modern complex that contains all of the best equipment, but the challenge is the same: excellence has no par.

In Athens in 1896, an American who was entered in the shot put went into the discus for the first time and, to everyone's amazement, threw his discus some 6 inches (15.2 cm) farther than the expected Greek champion.

At the Berlin Olympics of 1936, amidst Hitler's prewar racial rumblings, a black American athlete chalked up four gold medals, his previously set record in the long jump lasting twenty-four years.

In 1948 a thirty-year-old mother of two, nicknamed the "Flying Dutchwoman," captured the world's attention with four sprinting and hurdling victories.

The marathon is as old as the Olympics.
Here, in Mexico City, troops lined the route.

And in 1960, in Rome, an American girl, called the darling of the Olympics, won three gold medals, despite the fact that she had been bedridden for four years in her childhood.

These are just a few of the fascinating stories to be told about the Olympics. The thrill of the unexpected, the excitement of the unpredictable, the joy of the unbelievable; since the desire to achieve is ever innate in men and women, it is this spirit that drives them beyond the normal limits of their capabilities.

The marathon is one of the dominant and most picturesque features of the Games. In 490 B.C., when the Greeks drove attacking Persians back to the sea, a messenger sped on foot from Marathon to Athens, carrying news of the victory. It was a very long distance, and, parched and bleeding from the effort as he entered the city, the runner gasped out his message and died. The modern marathon is an event that remembers this soldier and athlete.

Acts of heroism in this event are as numerous as the list of winners; it is the toughest of athletic contests, requiring courage and stamina, and victory can be found in just completing the race. In 1896 a shepherd from the Greek hillsides dreamed of bringing glory to his country by winning the marathon. While other runners faded in the intense heat, the little shepherd plodded steadily on and at last brought the cheering crowd to their feet as he led the way into the stadium. He won for the glory of his country and realized his dream—a determined little runner had again brought victory to Athens.

It is of some concern to many people that political and domestic quarrels are inevitably part of recent Olympic contests. Today's advanced technology and economic burdens have pushed ahead of modern morals, and international hostilities are not uncommon. But if the Olympic Games are to survive in our time, all people in the participating countries will have to declare an open and honest friendliness to themselves and to others, and the importance of integrity and amateurism must be reestablished. Perhaps in the future our moral values will catch up with our materialistic progress, and the Games will once again be cause for world peace.

And people everywhere, track and field athletes included, must remember the words that de Coubertin said when he called for the restoration of the Olympic Games: "The important thing in the Olympic Games is not winning, but taking part. The essential thing in life is not conquering, but fighting well."

THE CHALLENGE HAS MANY FACES

With well over forty events listed under the heading of track and field, there is a discipline for almost every type of athlete and almost every interest. Some require immense power and strength while others involve agility and quick reactions. Some, like the sprints, are expressions of pure speed, and still others are highly technical events, demanding years of study and practice.

But as diverse and different as these events may appear, there is one thing that they share, one thing they all hold in common. Every athlete, whatever the age, sex, or ability, enjoys what he or she is doing. A dedication and desire of enormous proportions is needed to become an Olympic competitor, but that inner strength comes only from a love for the sport and an enjoyment of success.

THROWING

At a track and field meet, the throwing events are marked by four separate and distinct disciplines. All involve the throwing, putting, heaving, or slinging of an implement into a designated zone, the competition lying in the achievement of the greatest distance.

The Discus

The discus, a flat, circular disc of metal and wood weighing no less than 4 pounds, 6½ ounces (2.0 kg) for senior men, is flung from a circle that measures 8 feet, 2½ inches (2.5 m) across. The secret to success in this event lies in getting the discus to plane out during its flight so that there is a minimum of air resistance. Here, as in all of the throws, strength and good style are of utmost importance; if either of these is lacking, then the thrower will be limited in his or her accomplishments.

A discus thrower may assume any position desired, but most throwers begin by facing away from the field. They then spin across the circle one and a half times, holding the discus flat and away from their bodies, accelerating it as they move, and fling it as far as they can, once the turns are completed. To be counted as a good throw the implement must land in a sector that measures 45° from the midpoint of the throwing circle. For this reason, a beginner should probably start by using a simple standing throw in order to learn the basic technique; once accomplished, they can move on to more advanced methods.

The Shot

The shot is a heavy metal ball and, like the discus, is thrown from a circle, though a slightly smaller one measuring 7 feet

(2.1 m) in diameter. Junior athletes use a 12 pound (5.4 kg) shot, and senior men and women use the 16 pound (7.3 kg) and 8 pound, 13 ounce (4.0 kg) shots respectively.

Obviously, a metal ball of such weight cannot be thrown in the conventional sense as, say, a baseball or cricket ball would be thrown. Instead it is "put" from the shoulder using only one hand, the entire body being used to give force to the throw. Shot-putters, too, begin their throws by facing away from the "fair throw" sector and glide across the circle to gain momentum. Put properly, a shot might go as far as 70 feet (21.3 m).

The Javelin

The javelin is, essentially, nothing more than a modern spear and as such should be handled carefully at all times. And again, it should be stressed that it cannot be thrown effectively, as with the shot and discus, by using only the arm; one's entire body is used to maximize the distance achieved.

A women's javelin weighs 600 grams (21.2 oz) and is between 7 feet, 2½ inches and 7 feet, 6½ inches (2.2 and 2.3 m) long from tip to tip; the men's weighs 800 grams (28.2 oz) and is 8 feet, 6¼ inches to 8 feet, 10¼ inches (2.6 to 2.7 m) long. In throwing this implement a run-up approach is used, and it must be released from behind a "scratch line"; should an athlete cross this line during his or her throw, the judge declares a foul and the throw does not count.

A world record javelin
throw about to be released.

The Hammer

Only men compete in the last of the throwing events: the hammer. The hammer consists of a metal ball connected to a handle by a metal wire, the whole thing weighing 16 pounds (7.3 kg) and measuring close to 4 feet (1.2 m) in length. Holding the handle with both hands, a hammer thrower spins several times and moves across the circle (also measuring 7 feet [2.1 m] in diameter), accelerating the implement as he goes. Handled in the correct fashion, a hammer may go well over 200 feet (61.0 m).

THE JUMPING EVENTS

There are two jumping events for women track and field athletes, four for men. The basis of these events, of course, lies in one's ability to lift oneself off the ground, and as such, a good deal of a beginner's success will lie in powerful legs and good speed.

The high jump and long jump, in which athletes of both sexes compete, are fairly simple events, but a few comments may prove useful.

The High Jump

Two techniques are employed by world class high jumpers, the straddle and the "flop." The flop became the dominant style in 1968 when the American, Dick Fosbury, perfected a technique in which he approached the bar with a semicircular run and soared over the bar backwards.

More recently, however, the straddle, in which a jumper "rolls" over the bar face down, has regained its former premier status, as this method has been used in achieving the world records in both the women's and men's competition.

The Long Jump

The long jump is a very basic event; almost everyone has, for some reason, used the spring from his or her legs to jump from one place to another. Using as long an approach run as is required, the jumper must approach the landing pit, which is made of sand, from a designated direction, initiate the jump from one foot, and take off from a foul board—the jumper may step on the board, but no part of her or his foot may go beyond the side nearer the pit. Should the jumper's foot go past this board, a foul is declared and the jump is disallowed, the athlete losing a turn.

The Triple Jump

The triple jump is probably best described by its former name, the hop-step-and-jump. Using an approach run similar to that of a long jumper, the triple jumper seeks prowess in the ability to combine three different steps to achieve the greatest distance. The first jump, the hop, is achieved by taking off and landing on the same foot. From there the jumper takes an extended step onto the other foot, and completes the effort by then leaping off this foot and stretching into the pit, landing on both feet. Best results will usually be obtained if the jumper tries to make each phase of the jump as long as the next. While the movement is difficult to describe, it has a natural feel or rhythm when put to practice.

The Pole Vault

One of the most popular events is the pole vault. While an accomplished vaulter may make as many as sixteen distinct moves in one second during the peak of the jump, the basic motions are fairly simple and lots of fun to learn. Whether using a pole made of synthetic material as the Olympians do or the metal pole that beginners use, the pole-vaulter tries to get as much vertical height as possible, using the pole as a support and arching one's body over a bar that is resting between two standards. Pole-vaulters are among the best conditioned athletes at any meet since they use virtually their entire bodies to complete each vault.

DISTANCE RUNNING

There is no single quality that binds all distance runners together, unless, perhaps, it is the simple joy they feel in moving, unaided, across the earth. A distance runner spends hours training every day, striding alone through mile after mile, trying continuously to pull a few more ounces of strength from his or her thin, well-toned body. And it is a lonely sport, one that requires the union of body and soul, a spirit that cannot be dampened. Courage, both mental and physical, is the bread and water of a distance runner's diet—without it the athlete cannot persist.

In any discussion about distance running it is important to realize that we are dealing with a realm entirely different from any that has come before. In no other phase of track and field does the athlete have to withstand the relentless punishment that comes from the sustained, driving effort demanded by these lengthy contests. Jumping, throwing, and sprinting all involve quick, explosive bursts of energy that take anywhere from fractions of a second to several times that. But distance running alone tests stamina, resistance to pain, and the capacity to endure.

Both men and women run what are considered to be the "middle distance" events, competitions that require stamina and strength, but in which speed is also a key factor. These events, the 880 yard (0.8 km) run (covering 2 laps of the track) and the one mile (1.6 km) run (4 laps), usually have a limited number of competitors, which keeps the contact between runners to a minimum. Strategy plays a very important part in each race; a runner must be aware, not only of his or her own capabilities, but of an opponent's abilities as well.

The longer distance events, which have most often been limited in competition to men, are slowly becoming accepted as being women's races too. The Olympic distances of 5,000 m (3.1 miles) (12½ laps) and 10,000 m (6.2 miles) (25 laps) are run on the track. Quite a few runners are allowed to enter, however, since there is little inter-athlete contact in races of these lengths. Strategy is important here as well, and good pace judgment is essential.

The Marathon

One of the most demanding of all athletic competitions anywhere is the marathon, a race 26 miles, 385 yards (42.2 km) long. Marathon runners, usually thin and slightly built, are some of the world's most superbly conditioned athletes, and they can maintain impressive speeds over the entire course. Most marathon races begin on the track, where the runners complete several laps. They then leave the stadium and run the next 25 miles (40.2 km) or so through the surrounding streets, returning to end the race with a few final laps back on the track. Indeed, the highlight of most Olympic track and field meets comes when the marathoners reenter the stadium, exhausted and weary, but knowing that there is victory simply in finishing a race of this distance.

SPRINTING

Sprinters draw less on stamina and endurance and base their prowess on quick reactions, strong legs, and the complex

ability to use every muscle in a coordinated effort to propel their bodies forward as fast as possible.

Both men and women compete in the sprints, which are usually contested over 100 yards (91.4 m), 220 yards (201.3 m) (½ of a lap), and 440 yards (402.6 m) (1 complete lap). These races are run in lanes and generally require a maximum effort from the sound of the gun until the finish line is crossed. Young runners will probably find that 440 yards (402.6 m) is a long way to sprint and they will have to "pace" themselves, but a little practice at this will reap a big early improvement.

Most sprinters make use of "starting blocks," which, when securely fastened to the ground, provide a good brace for the runners' initial push. As the starter commands the runners to go to their marks, the athletes approach the starting line and crouch into the blocks. At this point, head bowed, concentrating, the runner has both hands, both feet, and one knee on the ground. When commanded to "get set" each sprinter lifts his or her knee so that the balance of weight is forward on the hands. And finally, when all the runners have come to the "set" position, motionless in their blocks, the starter fires his gun, the sprinters exploding down their lanes.

The sprinter—a study in speed and concentration.

Above: American high jumper
Dwight Stones shows his form.
Below: these women are competing
for a place on the Olympic team.

There are several events that still need to be mentioned but have been left out of the above classifications because they merit special attention.

THE HURDLES

Ten barriers, placed at regular intervals (10 yards [9.1 m] between flights) mark an interesting race called the 110 m (331.4 ft) hurdles. No penalty is declared if a runner hits or knocks down one or more of the hurdles, which measure 3 feet, 6 inches (106.7 cm) for men and 2 feet, 9 inches (83.8 cm) for women, but clearance is important because a brush with a hurdle will slow a runner down. While the skill involved in good hurdling is immense, an athlete accomplished at this event will look very smooth, almost fluid, en route to the finish line.

Take the same ten hurdles, lower them slightly and set them around the entire length of the track, spaced evenly, and the race becomes the 440 yard (402.6 m) intermediate hurdle. Run in lanes, as is the shorter race, this is one of the toughest of all track and field events.

Just short of two miles in length, the 3,000 m steeplechase is a variation of hurdling over a greater distance. Each of the twenty-eight barriers is 3 feet (0.9 m) high and sturdy enough to be stepped on, unlike the hurdles found in the

Getting out of the blocks quickly is extremely important to the sprinter.

shorter races, which will fall over when hit. An added feature of this event is that seven of the barriers (1 per lap) are accompanied by 12 feet (3.6 m) of water on the far side; to clear this steeple efficiently, an athlete must step on top of the barrier and jump over as much of the water as possible.

THE DECATHLON AND THE PENTATHLON

Most major championship track and field meets schedule competition in the decathlon (which stands for 10 events) for men and the pentathlon (5 events) for women. The decathlon takes a competitor through two days of hard, exhausting exercise as he competes in the 100 m (328.1 ft) race, long jump, shot put, high jump, and 400 m (1312.4 ft) race on the first day, the 110 m (331.4 ft) hurdles, discus, pole vault, javelin, and 1,500 m (4,921.5 ft) race on the second. The women compete in the 100 m (328.1 ft) hurdles, shot put, high jump, long jump, and 800 m (2,624.8 ft) race. Each athlete is scored on his or her performance by an internationally accepted table, which rates the athletes against world standards. As a word of caution, let no athlete enter one of these competitions lightly —it is tough, fatiguing work!

THE WALKING RACES

Comical in appearance but tiring in practice, the walking races are enjoying a bit of a revival in popularity. Walking is,

A walking racer practices.

basically, the same motion that we all experience, but there are several rules that accompany the event, the breaking of which can result in the disqualification of a competitor; at least one foot must always be in contact with the ground, and the leg must be straight as it passes beneath the body. While the motion looks exaggerated and awkward, a beginner may soon realize that this stride is both smooth and efficient for a race of over 20 km (12.4 miles).

RELAY

Track and field meets cater most often to the individual, pitting thrower against thrower, vaulter against vaulter. But the schedule does provide for team competition in the form of relays, which are as exciting as any event yet mentioned. One race, the 4 × 110 yard (100.5 m) relay, which tests several teams of four runners, usually opens a track meet. The other relay, the 4 × 440 yard (402.6 m) race, most often provides a fitting climax to a meet.

The baton, a metal cylinder 12 inches (30.5 cm) long, is passed between each of the four runners comprising the delicate "exchange" phase of these races. If this is not done quickly and effectively, valuable time is lost, and an outgoing runner may not complete his or her leg of the race if the baton is not in hand. All told, the relays provide an exciting, competitive start and finish to any track and field contest.

POTPOURRI

A few things still need to be mentioned in order to give you a complete picture of this sport. Perhaps you have noticed that sometimes in this book distances have been given first in metric measurements, while at other times inches, feet, and yards have been used first. This conflict is a result of the fact that track and field is truly a worldwide sport, and different units of measurement are used in different countries.

The United States is one of only a few countries that rely almost entirely on the imperial system, that involving feet and inches as the basic units. Most of the rest of the world, including Britain, uses the metric system, making results easily understood from one country to the next. The difference in the two systems is not great enough, however, to cause too much difficulty.

American tracks usually measure exactly a quarter mile

(0.4 km) around, or 440 yards, while tracks in other parts of the world are 400 m in length; the total difference in length is just under 3 yards (2.7 m).

Most races in countries of opposing systems are almost equivalent in length though, so that competition distances are as close to internationally accepted standards as possible. For example, Americans compete in the one mile (1.6 km) run while most countries race over the Olympic distance of 1,500 m (0.93 miles). But the difference in the length of these two races is only about 120 yards (109.7 m). Similarly, 5,000 m equates roughly to the American distance of 3 miles, and 10,000 m is only slightly longer than the 6-mile race that is popular in America.

It should also be pointed out that international competitions, including the Olympics, are always run using the metric system.

Track and field is, basically, an outdoor sport and is limited by the nature of competition to the warm months; in most countries, events are held in the summer only. Recently, however, competition has moved indoors during the cold winter and spring seasons, and athletes have found a new venue for their sport.

Indoor track is as exciting as the outdoor version, despite the drawbacks of confinement to a smaller arena. The size of the track will depend, of course, on the building that houses it, but most indoor ovals are between 150 and 220 yards (137.1 and 201.2 m) around. This means that more laps have to be run in order to complete a given race, but it also allows the spectators a closer view of the competition, which adds to the excitement.

As a rule, indoor times are not as fast as those achieved

outdoors since the smaller tracks mean sharper corners that are difficult to negotiate at high speeds. The field events do not suffer too much from space limitations though, and indoor records in these events often approach those set outdoors.

TACTICS

A few words on tactics might be helpful at this point. It will become obvious to even the most casual observer that the shortest route around the track is on the inside lane, and an athlete should stay near the inside where competition permits. (In some races the contestants must stay in their lanes, but the starting positions are "staggered" so that the outside runner is not at a disadvantage.)

Distance runners may also find that leading a race is tougher than following. Should this be the case, the athlete should try to stay as close to the lead runner as possible so that a finishing sprint is not in vain, while maintaining a position near the inside rail.

High-jumpers and pole-vaulters will appreciate that their disciplines are tiring. Winners in these events are judged by the highest jump completed, and as such, the jumper should pass at the lower heights and save her or his strength for the tougher, higher attempts.

Sprinters should be aware, too, that a good start is going to be an asset to a good race. Most competitions allow a sprinter at least one "false start"—running from the blocks before the gun is fired. If an athlete "jumps" the gun, the runners are called back to the starting line and the race is started anew. You should know, however, that two false starts will result in the disqualification of the guilty contestant.

Traditionally, all track races have been timed by a tier of officials who sit near the finish line and use stopwatches. These watches can accurately time a race and give the results in tenths of a second.

More recently, though, a new method of timing has been developed that involves the use of an automatic timing system and a camera, with results coming in hundredths of a second. While this method is more consistently accurate than hand timing, it is quite expensive, and is usually affordable only for major competitions.

BEYOND
THE TRACK

Beneath the huge slabs of concrete and plexiglass that rise as a monument to the University of Texas football team, a small group of athletes gathers for some of the most bizarre training in the sporting world. They are small in number, but among them are a couple of national champions in the shot put and discus; they are enormous men weighing in excess of 250 pounds (113.4 kg).

Together they push and pull, strain and shove, on weights exceeding 500 pounds (226.8 kg). They yell at each other when they fail to make a lift and applaud when they succeed. Their bodies ripple with each movement, their muscles appearing distinct and powerful. On the field during competition they are foes; during training they are the best of friends.

In Japan a strong, tall woman bends to touch her toes and then rises again to look at the horizon. This is a ritual she must perform every day if her muscles are to be stretched enough for her to run effectively. She knows that every muscle in her body must be in tune with the next or she has no chance of reaching perfection.

She continues to stretch in this manner for about thirty minutes, then jogs to a cinder track and begins to run as fast as she can, concentrating entirely on her forward motion. She stops her sprint after about 200 yards (183 m) and jogs back to her starting position. Arriving there, she turns and is off again. This woman is a sprinter, one of her nation's best.

In Uganda, a slender, bony figure emerges from a grass hut and trots slowly down a path, across a field, and into the forest beyond. Clad in shorts and some dirty running shoes that are worn at the edges, the runner begins a long climb to the top of the valley. As he starts the upward trek, a few beads of sweat pool on his cheeks, then slide to his chin and, finally, plunge onto his chest below. The path steepens; the pace quickens; his body responds and his heart answers the challenge.

The athletes mentioned here, and hundreds of thousands like them around the world, know that the only way to reach success is to train as often and as hard as possible. The only way to the top is through hard work, and one needs determination, sweat, and courage to remain there. Nevertheless, we need not forget one of the basic premises of this book: training must be enjoyable or there is no point to it, and the beginner in particular should be aware that a light workout load now will make a heavier session easier to handle at a later time.

SETTING UP A
TRAINING PROGRAM

The most important step in setting up a training plan, whatever the event, is to start running. Run in the park, down the street, around the football field. Run to school or to the shops and back home again. Jog in the morning down by a stream, in the evening as the sun sets, or run with the dog in the afternoon. An athlete should run whenever and wherever he or she wants, but the important thing is to run.

Two miles (3.2 km) a day will probably be enough to start off with, and an athlete can use this as a building block once this distance feels easy. Thinking up new ideas will keep the training from getting monotonous and boring, and you'll be building up a good background for further training. Running makes your heart stronger, your lungs bigger, and your legs more powerful, and every track and field athlete, regardless of the event, needs these things to start off with.

The next important step in planning training is to find a coach. Most schools have coaches and facilities available to the young athlete, but if this is not the case, there will probably be community organizations nearby. A coach will be able to help in the selection of an event to suit a particular athlete, will have ideas on how to improve one's training, and will be able to assist enormously on technical aspects. A good relationship with a coach is essential; he or she will provide inspiration when one needs support, comfort in defeat, and congratulations in victory.

Choosing an event follows obvious lines, but a few hints may ease some initial doubts. Distance runners are usually the smallest track and field athletes, mostly because it is easier to carry a small body over a long distance than it is a massive body. By the same token, for reasons that have to do with mechanics, strength, and physics, the throwing events usually require a husky, muscular body that is heavy by most standards. Sprinters and jumpers tend to lie somewhere in between, being solidly built but not oversized. Although your specific body type should not keep you from competing in an event that you like, your success may be limited by these physical boundaries.

Nevertheless, it cannot be said too often—do what you like to do. If you enjoy lifting heavy weights or throwing balls and rocks, then try your hand at the discus and shot. If you have a "feel" for jumping, then pursue the long and triple jumps. And if you simply like running as fast as your legs can go, then live the life of a sprinter.

But before you plunge headlong into a diet of running, jumping, and throwing, it should be mentioned that quantity is not as good as quality where training is concerned. Lots of hard work is essential to becoming a good athlete, but this should not be work without thought; a successful training scheme is an intelligent one. It is in this area that a coach is most helpful; he or she can help plan your training so that you are "building" properly.

The smart athlete, with or without a coach, will know that a medium amount of high quality training is better than an overload of poor training.

Every athlete must expect a little muscle soreness and a feeling of being "tight," especially during the early phases of training. For this reason, then, a good warm-up before a work-out or competition is a must. Some simple stretching like toe-touching, push-ups and trunk-twists, as well as a bit of jogging will loosen up sore muscles and prepare them for a heavier

Practice is essential for both amateurs and professionals to develop stamina.

load. The idea is to relax and work or "stretch out" the muscles so that they don't become strained or injured during the workout. For this reason, then, all stretching should be slow and smooth rather than fast and sudden.

Most athletes in track and field, particularly those in the throwing and jumping events, will need to do some kind of weight training. As with running, weight lifting should be approached with respect; take it easy at first, until you get a feeling for what you are doing. Care should be taken that you are not lifting too much weight, which might cause an injury. And most important of all, ask your coach to set up a scheme for you.

Everyone, especially athletes, should eat good, well-balanced meals. Strenuous sporting activities put an extra strain on your body, and a nutritious diet, rich in vitamins, protein (meat), and carbohydrates (potatoes and bread) will help your body in handling this extra load.

While there is no harm in training immediately after eating, some discomfort may be experienced by doing so. If this is the case, a couple of hours wait will usually clear things up.

EQUIPMENT AND CLOTHING

Finally, a word on equipment. Track and field athletes maintain that one advantage they have over athletes in most other sports is that their basic equipment consists of shoes, shorts, and a shirt—nothing else. Shoes, the most important part of an athlete's attire, should be comfortable, preferably with padding in the heels to reduce the shock of running on the athlete's legs and feet. While many of the best shoes are very expensive, there are shoes available that cost less without sacrificing much of the quality. They must also be well fitting and have good arch supports.

A warm-up or sweat suit will be helpful, particularly in colder weather, but once again, an expensive suit is not necessary. Young athletes must not be "psyched out" by other athletes who have expensive-looking uniforms and shoes; such uniforms tell of an athlete's wealth and not of his or her ability.

Running shoes are advisable for training and workouts, but often a different type of shoe is used during competition. Runners, jumpers, and some throwers prefer to have "spikes" or cleats on the bottom of their competition shoes. They might provide some slight advantage to a competitor, and will become important later on, but they, too, are a luxury that beginners need not concern themselves with.

Other equipment needed by throwers, jumpers, and hurdlers will probably be available through local school and community help.

KEEPING TRACK

Track and field is a sport of statistics and records; no performance would be meaningful unless there was some "yardstick" by which to measure it, some standard to compare it to. Record books are continually being edited and re-edited as every new season brings a host of improved performances, and a look at this sport would not be complete without at least a glance at some of these standards.

There are world records listed for every event in track and field as well as a multitude of other records that are of interest to the contestants on hand. There are, for example, national standards recorded for every country in the world. Age class records, high school records, state records, and event records are also maintained, to name just a few of the possible lists.

But there are other standards too, which, though receiving no official recognition, are generally accepted as being points of division. They divide the club runners from the international athletes and separate the good throwers from the great ones. They are marks that represent achievements in themselves and can act as respectable goals for athletes of any age.

The first and probably most famous of these unofficial barriers is the four-minute mile. Since the Englishman Roger Bannister first ran a sub four-minute mile in 1954, there have been a couple of hundred runners who have duplicated this feat. The four-minute mile remains, however, a goal that every miler strives for.

Likewise, an 18-foot (5.5-m) pole vault is considered to be a dividing point. And the list goes on: a 7 foot (2.1 m) high jump or a 26 foot (7.9 m) long jump; a throw of over 65 feet (19.8 m) in the shot put; 200 feet (60.9 m) in the discus; or a time of under 50 seconds in the intermediate hurdles.

Women, of course, have their standards too. Recently several women have run the marathon in under three hours, feats meriting a good deal of recognition. Similar honors lie in the high jumping of 6 feet (1.8 m), the long jumping of over 20 feet (6.1 m), and the running of 800 m (2,625 ft) in under two minutes.

As each athlete begins to consider which event he or she would like to compete in, these marks will become familiar and they will be respected as worthy goals. Yet athletes should also remember that they are not ends in themselves, for having reached these magic marks, they must try to go one step beyond.

On the following pages are listed some records that may interest young track and field athletes. These records are accurate as of the first day of January 1978. Junior records must be set by persons under twenty years of age.

WORLD RECORDS

EVENT	WOMEN	MEN
100 m	11.01 sec.	9.95 sec.
200 m	22.21 sec.	19.83 sec.
400 m	49.29 sec.	43.86 sec.
800 m	1 min., 54.9 sec.	1 min., 43.5 sec.
1,500 m	3 min., 56.0 sec.	3 min., 32.2 sec.
1 mile run	4 min., 29.5 sec.	3 min., 49.4 sec.
3,000 m	8 min., 27.1 sec.	7 min., 35.2 sec.
5,000 m	15 min., 37.0 sec.	13 min., 13.0 sec.
10,000 m	33 min., 15.1 sec.	27 min., 30.8 sec.
marathon	2 hrs., 34 min., 48 sec.	2 hrs., 08 min., 34 sec.
# high hurdles	12.59 sec.	13.24 sec.
400 hurdles	56.51 sec.	47.64 sec.
20 km walk	*****	1 hr., 24 min., 45 sec.
4 × 100 m relay	42.50 sec.	38.03 sec.
4 × 400 m relay	3 min., 19.2 sec.	2 min., 56.1 sec.
high jump	6′, 6″	7′, 7¼″
pole vault	*****	18′, 8¼″
long jump	22′, 11¼″	29′, 2½″
triple jump	*****	58′, 8¼″
shot put	73′, 2¾″	72′, 2¼″
discus throw	231′, 3″	232′, 6″
hammer throw	*****	260′, 2″
javelin throw	226′, 9″	310′, 4″
decathlon	*****	8,618 points
pentathlon	4,839 points	*****
steeplechase	*****	8 min., 8.0 sec.

***** Event not officially recognized
# Women run 100 m hurdles, men run 110 m hurdles

WORLD JUNIOR RECORDS

EVENT	WOMEN	MEN
100 m	11.13 sec.	10.11 sec.
200 m	22.73 sec.	20.22 sec.
400 m	49.77 sec.	45.04 sec.
* 800 m	2 min., 0.7 sec.	1 min., 44.9 sec.
1,500 m	4 min., 6.7 sec.	3 min., 36.1 sec.
1 mile run	*****	3 min., 51.3 sec.
3,000 m	8 min., 58.4 sec.	7 min., 43.2 sec.
5,000 m	*****	13 min., 37.4 sec.
10,000 m	*****	28 min., 32.8 sec.
marathon	2 hrs.,46 min., 23 sec.	2 hrs., 15 min., 36 sec.
# high hurdles	13.25 sec.	13.57 sec.
400 hurdles	58.61 sec.	49.61 sec.
4 × 100 m relay	44.05 sec.	39.69 sec.
4 × 400 m relay	3 min., 32.8 sec.	3 min., 4.8 sec.
high jump	6', 3½"	7', 7¾"
long jump	22', 22½"	27', 4¼"
triple jump	*****	57', 1"
pole vault	*****	17', 10"
shot put	63', 1"	69', ¾"
discus throw	207', 6"	203', 6"
hammer throw	*****	250', 7"
javelin throw	209', 6"	287', 11"
pentathlon	4,409 points	*****
decathlon	*****	8,124 points

***** Event not officially recognized
# Women run 100 m hurdles, men run 110 m hurdles
* Men's record is for 880 yards

AMERICAN JUNIOR RECORDS

EVENT	WOMEN	MEN
100 m	11.13 sec.	10.11 sec.
200 m	22.77 sec.	20.22 sec.
400 m	51.91 sec.	45.04 sec.
* 800 m	2 min., 0.7 sec.	1 min., 44.9 sec.
1,500 m	4 min., 16.8 sec.	3 min., 36.1 sec.
1 mile run	*****	3 min., 51.3 sec.
3,000 m	9 min., 8.6 sec.	7 min., 58.0 sec.
5,000 m	*****	13 min., 39.6 sec.
10,000 m	*****	28 min., 32.8 sec.
marathon	2 hrs., 46 min., 23 sec.	2 hrs., 17 min., 44 sec.
# high hurdles	13.50 sec.	13.57 sec.
400 hurdles	58.90 sec.	50.26 sec.
4 × 100 m relay	45.14 sec.	39.91 sec.
4 × 400 m relay	3 min., 37.9 sec.	3 min., 4.8 sec.
high jump	6', 1¾''	7', 3¾''
long jump	21', 7''	27', 4¼''
triple jump	*****	55', 1''
pole vault	*****	17', 10''
shot put	50', 3¾''	69', ¾''
discus throw	169', 2''	192', 8''
hammer throw	*****	203', 2''
javelin throw	198', 8''	273', 0''
pentathlon	4,005 points	*****
decathlon	*****	7,527 points

***** Event not officially recognized
# Women run 100 m hurdles, men run 110 m hurdles
* Men's record is for 880 yards

BOLD DREAMS

The number of great, dramatic performers in the history of track and field is impressive. Lasse Viren, Wilma Rudolph, Diane Jones-Konihowski, and Alberto Juantorena are only a few names from a long and substantial list. Each athlete has a story of struggle and victory, each a triumph beyond the track. And they all have one thing in common; for one moment, however fleeting or brief, each has attained greatness, grasped it, and held it aloft for the world to see.

Here are the stories of these four women and men:

Lasse Viren is now twenty-eight years old. He lives in the small Finnish town of Myrskyla where he was born, and started to run through the wide, peaceful countryside largely because there was nothing else to do. He went to school, of course, spent a while working for his father, and served a few months in the army. But through it all he ran, and his love for the sport gradually began to dominate his life.

It was while he was attending a mechanical trade school that he decided to commit himself full time to the realization of his goal, to win at the Olympic Games. So he quit the school, found a former runner to coach him, and ran off in pursuit of his dream.

A very economical runner, Viren has an enormous capacity to transport oxygen from his lungs to his muscles. This capacity, plus the 150 miles (241.4 km) that he logs every week in training, has made him one of the greatest distance runners in the world.

In 1972, when the Olympic Games were held in Munich, Germany, Viren was little known and seldom feared. He had previously recorded some good times, and had, on occasion, won some important races, but officials expected no more than a good, honest effort from the thin, bearded athlete.

Viren and his coach had different plans, however. Together they discussed the strengths, weaknesses, and habits of all of his opponents and planned a strategy to maximize his chances. They timed his training schedule perfectly so that he would "peak" at just the right time, and they worked hard for years to strengthen his body.

And when the Olympics of 1972 rolled around, he was ready. He won the 10,000 m (6.2 mile) race in impressive fashion, outdistancing the best runners in the world, and gained respect from those who had previously doubted him. He was not content, though, with just one gold medal and he returned to the Olympic stadium a few days later to win the 5,000 m (3.1 mile) race.

Perhaps the most impressive part of his 10,000 m (6.2

mile) victory was that he fell in mid-race and lost close to 40 yards (36.6 m) on the rest of the field. But he scrambled back to his feet, regained the leading group of runners, and then sprinted to win, setting a new world record in doing so.

Then the slight man from Finland disappeared from track and field circles and returned to his home, content to wait for the next Olympic challenge. Working as a country policeman, he was able to take time off to run, and he continued to train as he had before, thinking only of the Montreal Olympics in 1976. He took a month off every year to train in a warmer climate and competed in the European Championships every summer, but never reached the form that he had displayed in Munich in 1972.

Never, that is, until the Olympic flame was once again rekindled. He repeated his fantastic victories in both the 5,000 and 10,000 m (3.1 and 6.2 mile) races and made believers out of the most skeptical sports fans. He had done what no other athlete has ever done and had proved that his wins in 1972 had been the products of hard work and not of luck.

Now the unexcitable, shy athlete lives with his wife and one child in a beautiful house that the people of the surrounding community have helped him buy. And, true to character, he runs, concentrating on the one thing that is now important to him, victory in Moscow in 1980.

Wilma Rudolph, at the age of twenty, weighing 130 pounds (59.0 kg), standing 5 feet, 11 inches (1.8 m) tall, and possessing long, lean legs, had the ideal body structure of a sprinter. An inner vitality, which, when released, sent her surging—almost floating—down the track, coupled with her physical ability, won her honors at home and abroad.

But for this black American girl from Tennessee, international acclaim came only at the end of a long, personal struggle against poor health, which she refused to give in to.

Born the fifth of eight children to Edward Rudolph and his second wife, Wilma lost the use of her left leg at the age of four when she became severely ill. But her mother massaged her leg every day, and by the time she was eight, she could walk with the help of a specially constructed boot. For the next three years her family encouraged a "never give up" spirit, working and playing with her, and when she was eleven she dispensed with her heavy boot for good.

She became an outstanding athlete at the all-black high school in Clarksville, where she attracted the attention of the track coach at Tennessee State University. He saw tremendous potential in the young girl and drove her to the University daily in the summer of 1957 to train her. She demonstrated her exceptional ability in competition several times that year.

Once again, however, Wilma became ill, this time after an operation to remove her tonsils. But she remembered what her family had taught her, and she fought her way back to health, resuming her training in time for the Olympic Games in Rome in 1960.

The struggle proved worthwhile; as a representative of the American team she won three gold medals and the hearts

Left: Lasse Viren as he won the 5,000 m race in the 1976 Montreal Olympics. Right: Wilma Rudolph winning the 1960, 200 m race.

of the spectators. Nicknamed "La Gazelle," she bettered the Olympic standard in the 200 m (656.2 ft) run, and won the 100 m (328.1 ft) event in 11 seconds flat, only eight-tenths of a second slower than the men's time. And, on the final day of competition, she anchored the women's 400 m (1,312.4 ft) relay, completing her sprinting reign by winning the event and setting a new world record.

Following her triumphs in the 1960 Olympiad, Wilma toured Europe before returning to the United States and the distinctions that awaited her. She won the United Press International "Athlete of the Year" award in a European poll and was recognized as the American "Female Athlete of the Year."

Wilma returned to Tennessee State University to resume her studies in elementary education, and, later in 1961, she married a fellow student, William Ward. But she continued to dominate the American sprinting scene for the next few months, both indoors and out, and captured the imaginations of people all over the country.

When Alberto Juantorena arrived at the Olympic Village in Montreal in 1976, he was, perhaps, the only man who really knew what he was capable of. When he left, officials stood in awe of his incredible achievements and his outspoken manner. Juantorena, a powerful, brash young Cuban, had challenged the world, and won.

Juantorena is a big man; his enormous, caramel-colored body rises to a height of 6 feet, 2 inches (1.9 m), and he weighs 185 pounds (86.2 kg). Looking at him, you could guess that he once played basketball, as he did for the Cuban National Junior team. But team officials, noting his tremendous oncourt speed, urged him to turn his attention to a sport that could better use his natural talent.

So track and field coaches took over the young man's training, and in 1972 they entered him in the Olympic 400 m (1,412.4 ft) event. Young Alberto did not make the finals, however, and returned to Cuba disappointed but well versed in international competition.

He was hospitalized in 1974 and 1975 for surgery on his left foot, missing many months of valuable training. Still, he recovered sufficiently to place second in the Pan-American Games later in 1975 and proved to himself that he had the mental and physical strength to continue competing on an international level.

Confident, fast, and very determined on the track, Juantorena has been nicknamed "The Horse" in recognition of his long, thundering strides and powerful upper body. His brawn, however, has not prevented him from developing a keen, probing mind that reflects the same ambition that is evident in his running. Both he and his wife are studying at the University of Havana, and Alberto will work in the field of economics when he graduates and is finished with athletics.

And it is exactly this drive for self-betterment that has made Juantorena the best middle-distance runner in the world today. The years following his defeat in the 1972 Olympics brought a new vitality to the Cuban's track and field interests, and he expanded his competitive targets to include the 800 m (2,624.8 ft) event as well as the 400 m (1,312.4 ft) race.

He shocked the sporting world in Montreal in 1976; he won the 800 m (2,624.8 ft) race with a world record time, and recorded the fastest time ever in sea-level competition with a win in the 400 m (1,312.4 ft) event a few days later. No one had ever before won these two events in Olympic competition, and his accomplishment is often regarded as one of the greatest feats in Olympic history.

So pleased was he with his 800 m (2,624.8 ft) victory that he presented his gold medal to his country's president, Fidel Castro.

Juantorena once worked in a sugar factory and spent some time serving in Cuba's army. But he has now become one of his country's privileged citizens, living in a new house and driving a car that is equipped with a stereo tape-deck (he is inclined to listen to very loud disco music). His success has made him a national hero and an inspiration to the youth of his country.

He has, nevertheless, been robbed of his privacy, since he is constantly pressed for autographs at home and in Europe. Juantorena is far from shy, and he obliges his fans whenever possible. But even he needs time to himself—he'll have to concentrate if he hopes to defend his Olympic titles in 1980.

Like Alberto Juantorena, Diane Jones-Konihowski began her athletic career by participating in a sport other than track and field. While growing up in the Canadian province of Saskatchewan, Diane became involved in many aspects of artistic and physical activities, and at one time was ready to play on Canada's national volleyball team. And, as Juantorena, her abilities were rechanneled into track and field on the advice of a high school coach.

With his encouragement she made the national team in the high jump before she left school; but she agreed with her coach that she was better as an individual performer than as a member of a team. This way, she explains, ". . . if I win, it's on my own, and if I lose, I've only got myself to blame."

She continued her education at the University of Saskatchewan and spent a good deal of her time in track and field competition, entering every event that she had time for. It became apparent that, while she was very good in most events, she could make the most of her abilities by combining five of those events and competing in the pentathlon. At 5 feet, 10½ inches (1.8 m) and 153 pounds (69.4 kg), her main assets were strength and endurance, which accounted for her success in the 100 m (328.1 ft) hurdles, the shot put, the high jump, and the long jump. And, while her running has always been the poorest part of her competitions, she is improving steadily with good coaching.

As with many Canadian athletes, financial difficulties and a lack of outdoor training during the long, cold winters have impeded her rise to the top. Added to that is the pressure that any country exerts on its top athletes; friends and communities depend on these athletes to compete well in international competition. Diane has seen this type of pressure destroy good athletes and, while she is confident of her abilities, she is bothered sometimes by her country's expectations.

Despite the difficulties, however, she has maintained an impressive record of achievements. In Mexico, in 1975, Diane won the gold medal in the Pan-American Games, and beat the East German world record holder in the spring of 1976 during a competition in Austria. And as recently as August of 1978 she set a new Commonwealth record by taking the gold medal at the Commonwealth Games in Edmonton, Canada.

She has failed on two occasions to win an Olympic medal

and is talking of retiring before the 1980 Olympics roll around. She is not, however, disappointed in herself. Prior to the 1976 Olympic Games she said, "I'll be content and tell myself Diane is a success if I put out 100 percent. Should that give me a medal, fine, if not, then the other girls are better than I am . . . on this day. But if I know I haven't put out my best, then I'll know I'm not a success."

You can bet that Diane Jones-Konihowski put out 100 percent.

Diane Jones-Konihowski
jumps the hurdles in the
1975 Pan-American Games.

SOMETHING FOR EVERYBODY

There is no professionalism in track and field, no major leagues, no million dollar contracts. But that doesn't prevent an elaborate organization of events around the world, from the "little leagues" to masters' competitions, a reflection that track and field is truly a sport for everybody. There are events for the beginner who is just finding out about his or her abilities, as well as competitions for those with well-established talent. And, of course, there are international contests, with all their drama and excitement, for those of proven skill and dedication.

For the beginner, there are local events in every city across the country. Most schools have good track schemes and organized interschool championships. The enthusiastic athlete can reach virtually any level of competition.

*Local track and field organizations
encourage young people to train and compete.*

A young person interested in becoming involved in the world of track and field should first seek out local school and community organizations. Schools will almost always offer some type of training and should be approached first; they will probably be able to provide facilities, equipment and coaching, and their schemes will be geared toward the young athlete.

Community track clubs will have more quality coaching than school teams, but are probably interested in athletes that have gone beyond the beginner stage. These clubs should be approached, however, if local schools do not have facilities available.

Similarly, track events will be available through the schools during term-time, while the clubs will look after competition at other times. Besides a large number of local competitions that act as "warm-up" events, there will be larger events taking place across the country.

Universities provide for yet a higher degree of competition. And here, competition is usually fierce. The good and the strong survive, however, and some even represent their own countries in meets of international acclaim.

Beyond the universities lie the Pan-Pacific Games, the Commonwealth Games, the newly founded World Cup, and, of course, the Olympics, which are among the best sporting events in the world, and there can be no doubt that the latter two of these competitions are true global championships.

There is, then, something for everybody in the sport of track and field, and exploring the many possibilities is both exciting and challenging. Young athletes should not hesitate to become involved in this fabulous segment of the sporting world; the opportunities are immense, the fun never-ending.

SUGGESTED FURTHER READING

Coote, James. *History of the Olympics in Pictures.* London: Tom Stacey Ltd., 1972.

Durant, John. *Highlights of the Olympics.* New York: Hastings House, 1973.

McNab, Tom. *Athletics: Field Events.* Leicester, England: Brockhampton Press Ltd., 1972.

————. *Athletics: Track Events.* Leicester, England: Brockhampton Press Ltd., 1972.

Moore, Bobbie and Bowerman, W. J. *Track: Field Events.* Philadelphia: J. B. Lippincott Co., 1977.

BIBLIOGRAPHY

Christie, James. "Diane Jones Dreads Label of 'Sure Bet' Medalist." *The Globe and Mail* (Toronto) May 31, 1976.

Coote, James. *History of the Olympics in Pictures.* London: Tom Stacey Ltd., 1972.

Deford, Frank. "Heading for the 11th Event." *Sports Illustrated* August 9, 1976.

Durant, John. *Highlights of the Olympics.* New York: Hastings House, 1973.

Hendershott, Jon. "1976 Athlete of the Year, Alberto Juantorena." *Track and Field News* January, 1977.

Hill, Garry. "Alberto Juantorena." *Track and Field News* November 9, 1977.

Kieran, John and Daley, Arthur. *The Story of the Olympic Games.* Philadelphia: J. B. Lippincott Co., 1973.

Killanin, Lord and Rodda, John. *The Olympic Games.* London: Rainbird Reference Books Ltd., 1976.

Kirshenbaum, Jerry. "El Caballo Is Off and Running." *Sports Illustrated* August 29, 1977.

Le Masurier, John. *Hurdling.* Birmingham: Kings Norton Press, 1972.

MacGregor, Roy. "Pressure Times Five." *The Toronto Star* July 24, 1976.

McNab, Tom. *Athletics: Field Events.* Leicester, England: Brockhampton Press Ltd., 1972.

————. *Athletics: Track Events.* Leicester, England: Brockhampton Press Ltd., 1972.

————. *Triple Jump.* London: King and Jarrett Ltd., 1968.

McWhirter, Norris and Ross. *The Guinness Book of Olympic Records.* New York: Penguin Books, 1972.

Moore, Bobbie and Bowerman, W. J. *Track: Field Events.* Philadelphia: J. B. Lippincott Co., 1977.

Moore, Kenny. "An Enigma Wrapped in Glory." *Sports Illustrated* June 27, 1977.

Nelson, Bert. "Bruce Jenner." *Track and Field News* January, 1977.

Payne, Howard. *Hammer Throwing.* London and Tunbridge: Whitefriars Press Ltd., 1969.

Poole, Lynn and Gray. *History of the Ancient Olympic Games.* New York: Ivan Obolensky Inc., 1963.

Putnam, Pat. "Holy Moses, What a Dandy Race." *Sports Illustrated* August 2, 1976.

Sealy, Victor C. *How to Judge Field Events.* London: Amateur Athletic Assn., 1969.

INDEX